For my family and the LGBTQIA+ community

DEAR LIFE

A mistake that someone did put me on a chair
For all my life, and they don't even care
But in the end I see a glow
The beauty of my life I am here to show

My scars need no words
Of happiness I want to burst when it hurts
I am not on my own
Of my pain you will help me to let go when I come home

I learnt about my condition online
And it shows me that I am to be fine
If the world will be in on one motion
We will have a love explosion

My life isn't that sore
And it's healing like it was before
Your kisses
Are healing my wound like stitches

DEAR LIFE

The Christ is born
And I hope your sadness is all gone
Hoping that a smile is what you will wear
During all the year

Try to look in your soul
And make your anger go low
God is never mad
Even when you don't listen and act with your head

I just have to let you know
That god will never leave you alone
You need to do your best
And god will do the rest

I hope you feel happy and free
Like the beautiful Christmas tree
Let the snow fall
Happy Christmas and New Year to you all

DEAR LIFE

No matter if your white or black
Love won't hurt you behind you back
For the human beings who act like they are hard
And nothing can break them they need to take a look in their heart

In life you can stop crying
But you can't stop trying
When you feel down
And you are about to drown

Be careful because law trouble and bills
Is what kills
Before you do something you might regret think
Open your heart you never know some friends are passing from the same thing

To be free
Loving yourself is the key
Life is never fair
But a caring friend will be always there

5

Dear mummy
From the time I was in your tummy
You protected me
No matter how worried because of me you were to be

When I was born you asked the doctor how is my baby?
You then asked him will she live and he said maybe
You had a choice
You chose to give me a voice

You healed me whenever at school they beating me bad
You stood near my hospital bed
Lots of heartache
You had to take

No matter how much I let you down
You're with me still now
You taught me all the way
And you not once turned me away

DEAR LIFE

When I feel like a zero
You are my hero
Please don't ever let me go
But in you is where my heart finds home

Around me put your arm
To protect me from any harm
You always treated me right
And your beautiful smile is so bright

Your hand I want to hold
And I hope that together we grow old
You warm me up when I am cold
With you my dreams are being told

You thought me how not to be rough
From your love I will never have enough
You're the best
And anything like the rest

DEAR LIFE

From all the past
Is the happiness that last
Every day is history
But life is still a mystery

Life is full of love
Send from up above
The past is told
But the future is still unfold

When tears start to flow
Let your heart glow
War has no place
So let's live in pace

Life is full of joy
But it's up to you to enjoy

DEAR LIFE

Let me have this chance
To have this last dance
By this time
I know you can't be mine

I won't walk away
At the end of the day
I want to shout
I want pour my tears right out

When I think of you
And the pain in the deepness of my heart is all true
Your beautiful eyes
Can't hide all your lies

All our trust
When into dust

DEAR LIFE

My life hurts badly
I think I am going mad
My heart is full of pain
But I have no word to explain

Every time I see your face
My heart beat goes on a race
Being apart
Really hurts I wish I could be where you are

I tried to fill this emptiness
But without you in my life, I feel homeless
Every step that we made
Nobody can take

When you give your hand
There is anything to understand
You're the one that gets throw the day
And make everything okay

My life hurts badly
I think I am going mad

DEAR LIFE

You make my world
Just with a word
When I go to bed at night
You are the thing I have on my mind

I wish that I am the one you miss
And the only one you want to kiss
No I won't let you go
I didn't want to be on my own

When I see you my body stop breathing
Because my heart in love is bleeding
I miss you so bad
I can't get you off my head

To our dream we need to hold on
Before they are all gone

DEAR LIFE

I pray everyday
That your love for me won't fade away
Sometime you make me feel bad
But I still be the best you never had

I can't breath
Without you and me I get weak
I am not afraid
Because in our love I have the faith

We belong together
We will be ok as long as we have each other
In the moment like this
I can't let you miss

Love is not a game
 To see how many points you can gain!
Then you left so fast
That you made me put you in my past

DEAR LIFE

Like in the four seasons
I believe everything in life happens for a reason
You need to be strong
For all the trouble that comes along

I know they tried to break me
But I know that one day I will break free
You can never kill what you feel
All you can do is try to heal

Who I am I will stay
And evilness better get out of my way
I've given up
On the people that tell me I am not enough

To the sadness from past I am ready to let go
To abuse I am going to say no
With family and friends
I am going to continue my life plans

DEAR LIFE

I want to able to talk a bit louder
Of this world I want to be a bit prouder
Let them criticize
Till the real you realize

No need of a degree
Being judged hurts everyone and I think you agree?
I need to stop pretending
I know that life can be a happy ending

I need to stop being insecure
And to my sandiness find the cure
Everyone on this earth
Has some worth

Right now my life is tough
But I won't give up when it gets rough
With love and time
I know I am going to be fine

DEAR LIFE

When you lose all
To happiness you need to crawl
For others your life can be a taboo
 Just let it go and be you

Stop looking at the dark of the night
And start looking at the sunlight
If you stay strong on your side
Your life will never collide

When you say a lie
In your life there will be no light
If love is the case
Everything bad can be replaced

Sometimes life is hell
I know with the fake smile you couldn't tell
You need stop looking back
And find some friends that have your back

DEAR LIFE

My trust for you will die
If to me you say a lie
But my heart for you will still be beating
And from the love I have in my heart for you won't be leaving

My heart can't let you go
And you keep hurting because you know so
How to stop hurting I don't know
To you I can't say no

Your charm is your key
Over me
I don't want fame
I just want your heart flame

I wish you can give a second chance
And hold me in your hands
Without you I don't want to go far
Because I think of you as a superstar

DEAR LIFE

Even when walked out the door
My heart still wanted more
I will let my heart of this cage
And let this wound heal with age

I am sorry honey
Love can't be bought by money
I am not your toy
That you can just destroy

I need to say
Goodbye to the pain of yesterday
It's time to see the world now
And get out my feelings somehow

The beauty of life I want to see
Like the beautiful blue sea
I know that you are in a better place
But I still wish I can see your face

DEAR LIFE

I know I ended up in jail
And for you I am a fail
My life was one big lie
That made unable to feel free and fly

Our mistakes can take us anywhere
But the light of life will able there
With me I want to stay
I promise I won't run away

When everyone stare
It's like they are taking all the air
I want you to hear my heartbeat
And help get on my own two feet

I am going to take life slow
And let my heart to show
When to the ground I will fall
God will be my wall

DEAR LIFE

My heart is very clear
For you it will be always here
I breathe you at night
Of my life you are the light

I feel you like a sin
All over my skin
You are all I think about
You are the one I can't live without

I hear you in the echoes
I see you in the shadows
Do you remember?
That you promised a together forever

For you I can go throw fire
But for you I can't be a liar
I am not going insane
For feelings I can't explain

DEAR LIFE

In war
All you hear is pain full of roar
War is what man created
The people that loved are the ones that hated

When I go to bed
And close my eyes all I see in blood red
War destroyed everything forest and trees
Can only be found in my dreams

My son is at home
Praying for me not to die and leave him alone
I am waiting for the beautiful sun
So to my family I can run

My family love
Fits like a glove
Tonight we won't fight
And let the Christmas star bright light

DEAR LIFE

I am talking to you up there
Why are you taking from people who love her and care?
It's not like I can pay a fee
To make her pain free

Why would you harm
A person that for you has opened a loving arm
My family I can't see
Because the wide beautiful sea

You gave her pain from hell
To teach us a lesson well
I am knocking on your door
Because I can't see her in pain anymore

In winter you create the whites beautiful snow
Why to sickness you can't say no?
Just like a fallen leaf
Why can't you ask her pain to leave?

DEAR LIFE

You destroyed her life empire
With your selfish desire
A baby who isn't born
The soul of he or her you already torn

I found out I have a living being in me tonight
All my feelings are intertwined
I will help him grow on my two feet
In the hope that happiness we will meet

I will show our son
The beautiful light of life from the sun
I know my heart of pain will be bleeding
But that will never stop it from beating

Life isn't always a paradise
But I am ready to sacrifice
Piece by piece
I will bring my family some peace

DEAR LIFE

I hope that the world doesn't kill your childhood wonder
And that you will never suffer hunger
 I hope life doesn't treat you bad
And that you will always have a roof over your head

Poverty doesn't discriminate
No matter if you're hundred or eight
Life gave me a big shake
And to reality I am awake

Never forget from where you came
Of who you are never feel shame
Always give your family love and protection
And God will show you the right direction

Life can be a mess
Like a game of chess
I hope that you never feel emptiness
And that it will feel of happiness

DEAR LIFE

Cancer is a thief
A sickness that doesn't want to leave
Go on baby cry a human being can't be a stone
My fight to live has grown

Father, mother, sister or brother
We will be strong together and love each other
When you're in pain think of the beautiful weathers
Think of an angel with the snow white feathers

Imagine a sunny day
When you the sky in your life is grey
The people who love will help with sorrow
And you see a better tomorrow

 I hope that you know what happiness really means
And that the scars that the cancer left will never stop you to reach your dreams
 To help you though your dream is what I am here for
And I couldn't ask for more

DEAR LIFE

I am scared your heart will run to the ceiling
With all your beautiful feeling
You are so sweet
You make my day complete

You are a friend
That was Godsend
I know that when things get hard
You will give a piece of your heart

You are so kind
A friend like you is hard to find
Near you is where I am going to be
When you will need me

You are butterfly with strong wings
That with an inter force won over some difficult things

I am scared your heart will run to the ceiling
With all your beautiful feeling

DEAR LIFE

You broke my life to the root
In my heart you were ready to shoot
Jealously is what wins in the dessert drought
But caring words is what will come out of my mouth

Like a left behind dog
You left me in the blinding winter fog
True friendship will never sink
It is the type of love that can be written in your heart with ink

Our friendship is forbidden
My care for you will never stop I will just be hidden
I looked for you from east to west
But couldn't find you so all I can do is put my heart to rest

Even if of our friendship she took the spot
I am going to miss you a lot
I hope evilness to you she won't stir
Because you left our friendship and chosen her

DEAR LIFE

A mother knows her daughter
As we all know that in the sea there is salty water
In winter the snow was falling
And when a daughter is hurt her mother she will be calling

Like at every night there is a moon
When there is trouble she will reassure you that everything will be alright soon
She doesn't need a sign or a flag
When of happiness you lack

She will always come to your aid
And her love will never fade
In the end she will glow will pride
When she will see you as a bride

For you she always was here
And now your family she will cheer

DEAR LIFE

No matter what's your body form
You can be a power storm
In beauty of the heart is what really goes
Like every unique rose

Everyone needs to be voiced
Everybody needs to be enjoyed
Her hair feels like it was made out of silk
Her beautiful skin as white as milk

For you she will have no feelings to spare
She will know all that in your life you had to bare
She will see you as prince
With no sins

She will follow were he went
And she will never leave you discontent
When your life will go hay wire
She will be the one that in your heart she will light the fire

DEAR LIFE

There was a horse
Who looked like a magical force?
He is always in first place
With all his grace

He is this beautiful beast
That his kingdom wants to have a feast
No need for a chase
He wins every race

On that May
Every being was waiting for him to say
My son will love you each
For help he will be the one to reach

Everyone will be heard
From the king of the jungle to the little bird
Our kingdom we will protect
And each other we will respect

DEAR LIFE

To my dad I was a doll
He held me up every time I would fall
For me he was my white knight
In a dark night

We went to fields full of evergreen
Like it has always been
Every time I see his face
All I picture is an amazing place

He is the person I want to hear speak
When I feel weak
He is the one that I follow
And the ugliness of life he helps me swallow

He will give a bit of own
Before I go to the unknown
Even with all the bitterness he had to feel
With life he always made a happy deal

DEAR LIFE

To my baby sister in pink
A lullaby I use to sing
We use to play in the grass
And my hand though your hair I use to pass

I sing with you on my lap
Your eyes heavy ready to nap
Once we saved a bird nest
And in your eyes I was the best

Enjoy when someone in your life entrees
But I hope that distance between us never centres
I hope that the same me lullaby you will hear
Coming from my voice to your ear

I hope that when you think of me for awhile
I will bring to you a smile
To you amazing things I will be able to show
I love you and I hope you know

DEAR LIFE

When I hear the peaceful rain
A bit of my childhood I regain
Of a colourful butterfly I watched the birth
And I gave it a welcome to this earth

A breath-taking view to sight
Of all colours and even white
I hope that us harming them they will never fear
Because the little ones they cheer

To nature you will care still
You fly on the flower at the hill
Every day you will wonder
I hope that with your peaceful moves you will help the world to be kinder

I can listen to you calm
When you come on my palm
Even if you can't talk
I see you every time I go for a walk

DEAR LIFE

A farmer with his bent double back
His fruits of labour in a sack
In the strong sun that can bring you to blindness
Those facial lines full of kindness

From the bees he makes honey
For his poor family to have a bit of money
He barely knows how to write his name
But to hard work there is no shame

He needed the love of his daughter
Like to live he needed water
He said, in my fields there is a black crow
That protects the vegetables that grow

When he thought he reached his dreams
But life is never as it seems
He saw a cat with a chain of gold around head
And his life became better than he ever had

DEAR LIFE

As they say never mix work with leisure
But every time I look in your eyes my heart fills with pleasure
I remember that day me on my feet
My ear to your chest listening to your heart beat

Your favourite dress I wore
And went at the same where we first met at the shore
But when you became a stranger
You put me in danger

For you to come back I implore
Your smell I use to adore
In my life you brought a joy
That I never felt by a boy

Even if our relationship was brief
You made feel free and light like a leaf

DEAR LIFE

You took my body and I am the one who will have to pay the price
I feel numb and cold as ice
It will take time for me to remove the mask
And for help to ask

I feel touching like a choking tie
I hope that one day that feeling would die
To heal it needs time
Of my life I want to be the prime

It's time stop asking why
It's time to be me and myself without a why
To be happy I will go to every length
And I believe I got the strength

My whole self I will searching
My life I will be recharging
I will never go back
To that place so black

DEAR LIFE

When I went to town
I felt like a queen with a crown
We went to the beach
And we felt like nothing was out of reach

The town we wend
Like the night will never end
Our heads didn't hurt yet
And I hope this night we will never regret

We hit the road
With only drinks to load
At the end of the night we had to hold to the wall
So on each other we wouldn't fall

The hangover of Monday
Was no fun day

DEAR LIFE

From most jobs I was spurn
Looking for a job with my head held high I would return
Inside some people I think there is some venom snake
To touch you and make shake

My dream I will follow
I will write till my fingers will swallow
A disability can be a work force
That's only if you accept of course

To work hard I am ready
Even if I see my future a bit unsteady
I can't lie sometimes I want to stay in the shade
Because I feel like the world is a hurting blade

Heartache we all have to endure
I hope one day for that we will find a cure
On worrying night I go on the lawn
Staring at the sky and thinking till dawn

DEAR LIFE

Life is race when you reach the finish line
You will be able to shine
But I will give you my hand
To help you stand

All your hell I am going to see
Because you and me is what's going to be
Your heart with happiness I am going to fill
Even when you won't want there I will stay still

I want to be your queen
Don't be scared for our love to be seen
I hope old will grow
And dream of years ago

I love you with every breath
Till we are apart by death

DEAR LIFE

I left you and you became my best mate
But I have more feelings than that but I have to keep them inside and that is what I hate
With only one look
I still can read you like a book

My feelings for you have never flown
And will never, that why I am here crying on my own
My heart for you will never range
Even if my life I had to change

You know me in every shape
And without you my heart sneeze like a grape
In my heart you left me marks
And when I talk about you I still have sparks

I wish I was your beautiful girl
Like a beautiful pearl
The future nobody knows
I need to have faith and see how life goes

DEAR LIFE

I need to get out of my shell
And try to live my life well
From my mistakes I want to learn
All that I can

I want to show that even if I am not a super model hot
To be successful I still got a shot
I am not saying life is going to be easy and plain
There will sun and rain

I have a head as strong as metal
But my heart as soft as a petal
Don't get me wrong I am not going to the moon
Any time soon

On your dream you can't sleep
Step by step with no leap

DEAR LIFE

When I go in a lake
With nature I feel awake
Nature has its beauty in procession
Every secret and its confession

I hope the soft voice of the birds I will never have to deny
In a way day of July
It's a treasure
That you can't measure

The power of the wind went it blows
The magic white carpet went it snows
When the trees to us bent
And all their life away went

The birds that sing like angel bells
And the peaceful sound of the water wells
 Global warming gave nature a shock
But it still stand as strong as a rock

DEAR LIFE

Love is like a seed
That to you I would like to feed
My heart I need to pause
Because it's beating like a racing horse

You just need to kiss my cheek
And leave unable to speak
You are so beautiful looking in your eyes in a sin
Your eyes show your kindness within

You are so wise
Your heart for the beauty in me has eyes
All of you I want to reach
All your great self to the world I want to peach

My heart was about to burst
When I saw you first
An angel came
And in heart planted your name

DEAR LIFE

My heart is in a breaking state
But in myself I got to have some fate
I am on my knees on the floor
Like many hurting times before

I have a dream in life
And that is to be a good wife
That way my heart can be serene
And be the happy I have always been

Like a white dove
To the ones close to me I want to give pure love
Family is a fruit
From which we all get our root

When the sky is grey
Family knows what to say
When I am sick
They come to my side very quick

DEAR LIFE

I know that getting of drugs isn't going to be sweet
But there is loving people around you that will you get on your feet
Of course it's going to be hard before you are flash and bones
Don't let me wake up and find you as cold as stone

When all you see is dark mist
Don't give up when you least think about it in a beautiful way life can twist
The light from your eyes I want to see beaming
Of the amazing stuff I want to be dreaming

Every day without drugs means a step to take control of your is nearer
And maybe your life issues will become clearer
Even if the heart of the ones that love you torn
From your life they will never be gone

When the pain you start to feel
You will start to heal
Drugs are a curse
That can only be broken by all the love in the universe

DEAR LIFE

You stole me and make me wear a mini shirt
So my body you will be able to hurt
For your sex pleasure you caused my unstoppable pain
All my future went in vain

All the beautiful things in life that I was about to plot
My heart had to forgot
I am shy of my name
Because of you I can never be the same

A human act
Can become a life fact
Some humans for their life need to fight
And risk their life to every height

Everyone has a story to tell
And I hope that the human trafficker end up in a prison cell

DEAR LIFE

At night when I put my head
On my bed
Thinking back when I was seventeen
All I saw is love and the nature forever green

After a few years started the home loan
And the bills ate me to the bone
Life can pass in a blink
But we all have life memories to link

But people can be hurt
And see only the world as dirt
The only way to cope
In life is to have hope

All we see is a hill
When we are ill
Our problem we all have to face
But we need to stay calm and do it with grace

DEAR LIFE

God gave me a kid as a gift
The only one that my day can lift
His life was about to start
Someone ending his life as an unfinished piece of art

 I feel like I am the one to blame
I can't even cry for my son because everybody thinks it's weak and lame
My heart is filled with rage
It's like they threw it in a tight cage

The heart of our family was cut to the core
And we don't know what he did it for!
There is no time for pleading
It's time to start leading

With life we have to deal
And I hope that my bleeding heart will seal

DEAR LIFE

They are going to put you in a jail cell
And they sent my heart in painful hell
I hope you find your heart at peace
And that your hate for others will not increase

For more pain there is no need
And that from my love you will feed
I will go to every length
To help you get back your strength

I go numb
Every time you say you are dumb
Please show that smile
That I haven't seen in a while

The pain I have will never kill
I will wait for you still
Let your eyes shine
When they look into mine

DEAR LIFE

Every time I think about you in brain
All I feel is pain
At times life feels like a maze
We all need to find our exit place

In life we to overcome shocks
That can be as hard as rocks
There will be moments when you feel like you are carrying a cross
Especially when you stuff loss

With time I hope you get some glow
Like angel wings white snow
Your voice will be able to sing
Like the colourful spring

Look at the bees in showers
To give live to the flowers
Nature magic they spray
For dead to go away

DEAR LIFE

You crossed that painful line
And that's not fine
Even if when I saw your back
My heart started to crack

We were one for a while
And when I think of our happy days I still smile
With that evil stare in your eyes I need to deal
Even when my heart still wants your feel

I hate when your anger goes wild
Like that of a small child
I know that in our relationship we never had the perfect ace
Never been the case

For you I was just a game
A few minutes of fame
I am done with your evil tongue
I am going to let my heart free and young

DEAR LIFE

You were my light
In the darkest night
You were there to help me stand tall
But still helped me when I fall

You helped me to get out of my shell
How much I love you to the world I want to tell
The pain I carry is curse
By losing you felt worse

We can't change our fate
But from our lives we can block the hate
Please give me your arm
To protect me from harm

You're my core
And I need nothing more

DEAR LIFE

Numb like a ghost
Pain is my heart host
You say you are a guy but I say you are a two year old boy
Because you are treating me like a toy

I am the woman with the crown
Because your evilness knocks you down
Don't ever forget who are
That's the thing that will get far

Keep your devotion
Because that what will keep your life in motion
Hurt isn't all that I am about
But it's a feeling I can't go without

Very deep
I have an ach I can't keep
Passion isn't something you can fake
And it will give you power with every step you take

DEAR LIFE

When all your happiness is out
Prayer is all that will count
In my heart
I want your mark

You are a legacy
In all my fantasy
When life makes have a confrontation
Your love has no limitation

You will help me follow
And you help me get ready for tomorrow
Your voice is what I heard
Without not even a one word

Even in nature you give us beautiful hints
Like the powerful winds
You know all of our regret
But you are the one that forgive and forget

DEAR LIFE

When you feel like you're at loss
And the bad way you are about to cross
When the monster within
Feels like he is about to win

I can see the shine in your eyes come through
Loving yourself is the first thing you have to do
Girl for your identity you have to fight
Your life is on the line

When you feel like you are alone and dirty
I will show you how much more you are worthy
Don't let your heart to shatter
For the people around you really matter

Your beautiful side
Has never died
I will never be alone
At home

DEAR LIFE

I will set our love on fire
Till I know you are no longer a liar
Even if my mind has more than one question
My heart can't stop giving you affection

You promised that my heart you won't break
I realised that that was fake
For me, you only felt lust
That went away so fast

This is me
And that's all I want to be
I am out
Fed up of the anger coming out of your mouth

I love you still
I hope you can climb that hard hill
I will live day by day
And let my feelings play

I will set our love on fire
Till I know you are no longer a liar

DEAR LIFE

There is a child that had to steal
For his meal
And I waste my food
Because to eat I wasn't in the mood

My home is a coffin
But I am kid in poverty so my voice isn't heard very often
I wish so bad to go to school
Because to get out of poverty education is the tool

But I will still sing
Thanks to God for every beautiful spring
My heart is clean
And I am not mean

To success I will ride
With all my pride
I will follow the sunny beam
And do my parents dream

DEAR LIFE

In morning I can hear my alarms
But I don't want to let go from my arms
When I watch sleep in peace
I know that of my heart you the keys

In my head I can see you bright
Our love from last night
When I look in your eyes so blue
My heart is yours and you have no clue

I will put your trouble lives aside
Because I have nothing to hide
Every scared line
On your body looks divine

When I am sad I hope to find your embrace
And that my heart will find its place

DEAR LIFE

I hope I can climb mountains
When my tears are falling like fountains
They say I was an error
But that makes me strong when I look in the mirror

From what you heard you created a bad name that with me is set
Even if we never met
Myself I am going to remain
Even if you hurt me again

My past I will never grief
Because now I can breathe relief
The love in my heart is a gift
That will never drift

I am part of the next generation
 And I am full of determination

DEAR LIFE

When you died you left me no breathe to spare
And a heart I can't share
You left in a city
That has very little pity

I am keeping my tears inside by a thread
Because I know I will always hear your lovely voice in my head
When I was a kid I came and ring your bell
When something sweet to you I wanted to tell

When in my life I have no doubt
You are the one I think about
You are my fire
And my life desire

She was there at full speed
When I was in need
And she always had ears
To listen to my fears

When you died you left me no breathe to spare
And a heart I can't share

DEAR LIFE

She is a fighter
And that makes my heart lighter
I am in love with her
But my heart she is ready to tear

I am a girl and I love her
From her toes to her hair
When my love for her I understood
I ran away from her as much as I could

She will never know the meaning
Of what I am feeling
But one day will see the light in the sun
And I won't have to run

When everyone is gone I will be here still
With my heart for you to fill
I hope that every day the really me
You will see

DEAR LIFE

My life is out of tune
And I hope my heart and soul will be together soon
My dreams
Are so far away from what it seems

You can't pretend
When you have feelings for your best friend
She is a girl
As special as a rare pearl

Life passes in a blur
Will our love occur?
You're holding my life's rope
Please give me some hope

You are my life rock
And you are my heart lock
What will be will be
Who knows maybe one day I will be on one knee

DEAR LIFE

You can have wealth
But what's the use if you can't have health
Money isn't how you measure
Life and its pleasure

Living is high leap
For a happy life to keep
Enjoy all the air
That your lungs will bare

Stop worrying about with whom you were seen
And what your past have been
Of your life be proud
Because you deserve with no doubt

The heart is the base
Of every life mace

DEAR LIFE

To my brother I had to wave bye
Even if I didn't know why
Your soul is full of light
Like an angel in white

My mum felt like they killed her with a gun
When they took away her first son
You give me your little hand
Because when I'm in trouble for me you always stand

I remember your hair so black
Without you, our hearts started to crack
You dying young
It felt like no air in my lung

To you being gone I will never get used
To forget you I refused
At times you are so wrapped in our own bubble
That we don't see the real trouble

Skylar I want to thank you
With your love I got through
This week my life was full of thunder
But you never let me go under

Your friendship is pure
And that was my cure
I want to let you know
That you are special from head to toe

Your heart has no hate
And that's what you great
You fight like a fighter
And that's what in life will get you higher

Don't ever stop
Till you reach your life top
Thanks for coming into my life
And cut my sadness with a knife

If you are thinking about cutting in your head
Think of how your family will feel when you are dead
You were given to earth
Because your life has a lot of worth

When you feel like you're on knees
Call help please
Phone your friends and they will be there
In a blare

It's going be to okay
Even if right now they don't accept you as gay
Say what need to say
Because they will listen to you one day

When your sky is grey
With you I am going to stay

I feel like I am living in a world full of lies
Because the real me I always disguise
Of my family I think
And what pain the real me would bring

My body and mind with pain are freezing
My loved ones are my heat and sense of reasoning
And they are the ones I will pick
Even if the pain makes me sick

You have the task
To see the real me behind the mask
Are you capable of that?
Or will you leave instead

Are okay will my dark hole
Or is breaking me is your goal?

When I tell people I am a boy
They treat me like a broken toy
When you're in the wrong body it feels like a cage
Full of fear and rage

I am transgender is what I will yell
One day my body will get out of this hell
Myself is hard to embrace
When I feel like an empty space

The real me I want to see bloom
Even if I had to walk to the moon
No more shame
When I hear my birth name

Enough with being numb
Happy times will come

I met a pansexual like me
I feel like our friendship was meant to be
Our friendship is strong like a rock
That nobody will be able to knock

I look in your eyes
And I know your soul hold no lies
With you a great friend I have received
And I know that from you I will never be deceive

Of making smile you have the power
And I know you will be there for me an hour
You saw my dark side and your here still
And that's a best friend skill

You were my escape
And the one that helped give my life some shape
You are with me when I am at ease
And you help my life go back to have some peace

DEAR LIFE

My mind to my body I can't connect
Of my body have little respect!
It makes me want to quit
Cause while fighting for my gender my heart in million pieces has spilt

I look up into the skies
And the boy inside me cries
Hurtful words is what you speak
But they aren't going to make me weak

You call me a fool
But being me is my fuel
You can be any gender
As long as your heart is tender

Of you I have no need
Because the love in my heart will give me speed

DEAR LIFE

No, I didn't want to be raped so I fought
But you didn't stop till what you wanted you got
An abuse that was never caught
But an evil act to me it taught

You saw me as trash
So my body you wanted to burn to ash
I felt dirty and no longer pure
Of my life, I wasn't really sure

I have a tougher skin
Than you think and I won't let you throw me in the bin
I hope you can live with what you did to me man
Because you left your mark in my life plan

My body you don't own
And if you passed the same as me for support you need to phone

DEAR LIFE

Because I am transgender she called me a liar
My pain inside me is like a burning fire
I felt like this for years
But to listen to me you never had ears

The one I love I never named
Even if she is the one you blamed
Of me you are ashamed
And at breaking my heart you always aimed

You call me your kid
But to my gender, you want to put a lid
Because you don't want your son
Of me, you will have none

Things aren't like they were
Cause I can't be any longer her

Because I am transgender she called me a liar
My pain inside me is like a burning fire

DEAR LIFE

You can try to disguise
But I will still see you through your eyes
My love to you is a never ending chain
Like a body vein

 Please stay
Because without you I am a lost stray
Without you everyday
My sky will be very grey

No rain
Will ever never my pain
All my happiness you always bring
And I hope one day you on your hand you will have my ring

Your name to me like a tattoo
Even when you don't have a clue
I want to be your sweater
In the cold weather

DEAR LIFE

Like dancing is like a dancer
Writing is my answer
A passion
That took me out of depression

When you feel all on your own
And all your friends are in the don't talking zone
When you feel like breaking every bone
Because your life is as hard as stone

When my friends say a lot of lies
But they don't know the pain that lies within
When life feels like a spell
That didn't end well

Carrying pain on your aching spine
That will alone heal with time
I am fed up of feeling cloaked
And in love I want to be soaked

Like dancing is like a dancer
Writing is my answer

DEAR LIFE

My best friend is a great guy
And that's something that nobody can deny
Someone that I can really count on
Because when I needed him he was never gone

Who kept strong!
Even when his family thought he was wrong
No matter what time
He listens and gets back in line

Be being he
He taught me the real me
Today I thought I lost him
And I felt like I lost a limb

I will be by your side
In this hard ride

DEAR LIFE

My mind says you can't eat
Anorexia took my life's front seat
My body is dying bit by bit
Feeling like it this world I no longer fit

No dead I won't let you hit
And that I need help I will admit
Break that invisible wall
Don't listen to that voice from the evil call

From darkness you will be able to rise
Because you are wise
To this earth
You're full of worth

I am going to leave this dark room
And the warm sun I want to costume

DEAR LIFE

Please don't leave
Because of my love you're the thief
I want you to know
That I will never let you go

Your love is like a beautiful drug
And I would give an arm for a hug
You make me see the light
When I am crying at night

You're all I need
You make my heart go an unknown speed
If you will be mine
My life will be more than fine

Of my pain you help me heal
Cause my heart you force to feel

DEAR LIFE

When you only see yourself through the ugly lens
When your muscles become all tense
And your life makes no sense
Like a hurting fence

When fall in a dark whole
Who will be there for me to console?
Please God remove the hate
And make the world in a better state

I pray that no one will feel like a waste
Because life is hard when faced
The way is long
But I will always come along

I won't let you put your life to smoke
Because the wrong words you spoke

DEAR LIFE

He is seeing the same stars
Even if he is behind bars
I am in jail
Because addiction made me fail

I am sorry for my kid
Cause he is the one who is paying for what I did
In this tiny cell
My really story I can't tell

People will always see my flaws
Because I touched with the laws
Society I will survive
Because my five year old needs me to be alive

I will make sure my son goes to school
Because school is a powerful tool

DEAR LIFE

Looking outside at the rain
Honey I can't get you out of my brain
When you wrote that note
It felt like left me at sea with a broken boat

I smell a nasty mist
Because my heart is in a twist
I can feel my despair
Still in the air

A drunk driver took him away from me
Help me forgive that's all I plea
I can still smell you on your side of the sheet
And can still feel your warm feet

Of that scene I had a dream
And I woke up with a scream

DEAR LIFE

Even when life gets hard as metal
I will treat you like a delicate petal
Your eyes are so pure and clear
I was you were here

I will hold you tight
Because for you I want to fight
On your heart I am going to put my palm
So you can keep me calm

Life isn't a game
But in the hard and easy parts I will love you the same
All of me you get
Since the first time we met

I know that your love
For me is enough